Investigating Maths

B O O K 1

**Robert Fisher
and Alan Vince**

Blackwell Education

First published 1988

Basil Blackwell Ltd
108 Cowley Road
Oxford OX4 1JF
UK

British Library Cataloguing in Publication Data

Fisher, Robert
  Investigating mathematics.
  Bk. 1
  1. Mathematics – For schools
  I. Title   II. Vince, Alan
  510

ISBN 0–631–90172–8

Designed and typeset by DP Press Ltd, Sevenoaks, Kent
Printed and bound in Great Britain
by Dotesios (Printers) Ltd, Bradford-on-Avon

Contents

Introduction

Investigating Maths contains a collection of problem-solving activities, puzzles and investigations for use in primary and middle schools.

- Books 1 and 2 are intended for the 6–10 year age range (top infants and lower juniors).
- Books 3 and 4 are intended for the 8–12 year age range (upper juniors).

The activities chosen are relevant to children of different ages and abilities.

Selection for each book has been based on (a) the notion of the spiral curriculum in which concepts are 'revisited' at ascending levels of abstraction, and (b) the need to introduce, in Books 1 and 2, the concepts and the investigational and problem-solving skills required for activities in Books 3 and 4.

There are 20 units or themes in each book. A unit consists of a double-page spread of teacher's notes and a pupils' worksheet which may be photocopied. Each unit presents adventurous and open-ended challenges to children, suitable for individual, group or class work. The investigations have been chosen and classroom-tested to provide mathematical challenge with sound mathematical content. There is a chart showing how the investigations fit into the framework of the mathematical curriculum, and at the end of each book is a record chart for teachers' use and resource sheets which may be photocopied for the pupils to use.

Investigating Maths has been designed to complement and enrich any school mathematics scheme. The suggested activities may be adapted to suit the style of individual teachers and the needs of individual children. The series is a flexible resource which:

- provides a rich source of stimulating mathematical activities,
- can involve pupils in investigations of their own choice,
- is suitable for group work on a particular theme,
- offers ideas and starting-points for class teaching, and
- fits naturally into any core scheme.

Each investigation provides a stimulus for further mathematical study. The teacher's notes describe the *equipment* to be used, the *facts*, *skills* and *concepts* involved, *teaching points* and ways of *extending the investigation*. The units are cross-referenced to show links, continuities and developments in *related investigations*. The activities can be developed in different ways to provide mathematical experience at many levels.

Aims and objectives of the activities

Each activity in *Investigating Maths* is designed to help children practise skills, understand concepts, and develop strategies for investigation. The teacher's notes give details of these for each activity. They also list any knowledge that the children need to bring to the activity, under the heading **Facts that will aid investigation**.

- **Skills** are the basic operations and routines to be tried and practised in the investigation, such as processes of calculation, use of calculator, measuring, problem-solving and investigational skills and strategies;
- **Concepts** are the principles underlying facts and skills, and how they are related; for example, equivalence, conservation, patterns – through abstraction, symbolisation and generalisation;
- **Strategies** are plans of approach to problems and investigations; for example, estimation, test-and-improve methods, simplifying a difficult task, looking for a pattern, reasoning, making and testing hypotheses, proving and disproving;
- **Personal qualities** are developed through this investigatory work; for example, being imaginative, systematic, independent, co-operative, persistent, playful and creative; and demonstrating the positive attitudes which assist learning.

Calculators

Calculators are often required in investigations to help facilitate a strategy of investigation. In predicting results, for example, tabulated number patterns may need to be extended, requiring a certain number of calculations. However, such calculations are only tools to aid investigation. Concentration on the method and practice of calculation may serve only to divert attention away from the development of a problem-solving strategy. We therefore recommend the use of calculators to help remove possible barriers to the free flow of ideas and the testing of strategies. The simplest of calculators will suffice, and they require only the minimum of skill. In addition, calculators can provide a means for children to explore their own mathematical thinking. Some activities have been designed with this in mind.

Problems, puzzles and investigations

Investigating Maths contains problems, puzzles and investigations. The terms 'investigations' and 'problems' are often used rather loosely. Problems and puzzles usually have a particular goal.[1] There is an obstacle, or series of obstacles, preventing the goal being reached immediately. The problem-solver must try a range of strategies to achieve the goal, and many of these strategies are investigational. An investigation is a process, including discussion and practical work, which may be used to solve problems or puzzles.

Investigations often have no immediate or obvious goal – just a range of results which may occur depending on the path being followed. An investigation is closely related to the concept of a 'game', and is similar in that it is given structure by the constraints of rules and materials. Many investigations are 'open-ended', open to a wide range of creative interpretations. Others, such as problems and puzzles, are 'closed' in the sense of having a specific objective or solution, but the process of achieving the goal may be 'open-ended', and once a solution is found many other extension paths may be followed. Extending the original investigation may produce new questions, new problems, new avenues of exploration.

The following model offers a rich learning experience in which the learner may enter actively at any stage.

stimulus → investigation → problems → extended investigation

variety of conclusions ← new problems ← new investigations

Using the book

The book may be used for individual, group or class lessons. However the book is used, it must be stressed that the pupils' worksheets only provide starting points for mathematical investigation. Each activity can be developed in different directions, at various levels, and ways of doing this are suggested in the teacher's notes.

The worksheets do not provide a scheme which needs to be 'worked through'. They offer a stimulus for children to develop their own lines of inquiry – with help from the teacher and from the group. The value of this work lies in challenging children to develop mathematical processes and strategies for themselves.

Look out for the following stages[2] when carrying out investigational work.

- **Entry** – getting to grips with the task either as individuals or as groups. Some children may need to see others at work in order to get themselves started. Questions you may ask include: 'What are you investigating?', 'Tell me about what you are doing,' and 'What are you going to do next?' Remember – sitting thinking, mulling over, is not a waste of time, it is vital to the learning process.
- **Attack** – tackling the problem, recording ideas, looking for patterns and relationships, guessing what happens next, trying a variety of methods using apparatus, diagrams, pictures and words. Questions include, 'How are you going to record what you find out?', 'What do you think?' and 'Why do you think that?'
- **Review** – testing the theory, predicting the outcome, checking the results. Questions: 'Does it work? . . . Why not?', 'What do you think will happen if . . .?', 'Can you explain what you did?'
- **Extension** – developing the investigation further, exploring other problems that occur, posing new problems. Questions: 'Can you try a different way?', 'What could you change?', 'What have you found out?'

What do you think?

Investigations should play a vital part in any mathematics curriculum, but how they are used depends much on the teaching style of the teacher and the learning of the child. Below are some issues for us, as teachers, to consider in preparation for an investigation.

Teacher attitudes
    Learn with the children
    Admit we don't know/can make mistakes
    Trust children to make their own decisions

    Intervene only when appropriate
    Encourage collaboration and discussion
    Accept a range of results
    Allow time for 'thinking things through'
    Reward children who are 'risk takers'

Classroom organisation
    Have basic equipment readily available
    Allow children to collect their own resources
    Arrange furniture for ease of movement and access
    Train children to return all equipment
    Encourage planned discussion
    Explain how they record results
    Make them clearly aware of your own role

Helping the children
    Encourage a systematic approach:

- **Strategies** – to look for patterns, test out ideas, simplify problems, try models with apparatus, diagrams, pictures, etc.
- **Organisational skills** – encourage thinking time, collaboration and communication
- **Investigational procedures** – stress the need to consider all factors, to record results, to estimate and to predict and visualise outcomes

Assessing the results

Establish a system for the child and the teacher to record the work done, e.g. on a record sheet or in a diary. The grid at the back of the book may help in the process of assessing what topics have been investigated.

In investigational work, problems and disappointments will arise, as will success and satisfaction. As Cockcroft said, 'The ability to solve problems is at the heart of mathematics.'[5] and in recognising and meeting this challenge teacher and pupils work together with *co-operation* and *mutual support*, just two of the qualities that we hope will be fostered by using this book.

Why investigate?

The need for investigative work in mathematics has been stressed in a number of recent official statements. The Cockcroft Report[3] argued that investigational work is of prime importance in the mathematical development of all children. The most famous section of the report – paragraph 243 – suggested that mathematics teaching at all levels should include opportunities for:

- exposition by the teacher,
- discussion between teacher and pupils and between pupils themselves,
- appropriate practical work,
- consolidation and practice of fundamental skills and routines,
- problem solving, including the application of mathematics to everyday situations, and
- investigational work.

The importance of investigational work is discussed more fully in paragraph 250, and an important message is given in paragraph 252:

2

It is necessary to realise that much of the value of an investigation can be lost unless the outcome of an investigation is discussed. Such discussion should include the consideration not only of the method which has been used and the results which have been obtained, but also of the false trails which have been made in the course of the investigation.

Investigations provide children with opportunities to engage in discussion and language related to mathematical activity. This talk can be of value in its three forms:

- the talking to oneself that comes from thinking aloud and trying to think things through;
- the discussion with others in a group setting, exploring ideas, sharing thoughts and suggesting avenues of inquiry; and
- the dialogue between teacher and child that stimulates thinking, the development of reasoning and the examination of alternatives.

According to the HMI Report *Mathematics from 5 to 16*,

> In an investigative approach pupils are encouraged to think of alternative strategies, to consider what would happen if a particular line of action were pursued, or to see whether certain changes would make any difference to the outcome. In fact, it might be through an investigative approach to a problem that a solution emerged. For example, if the problem is to find the most economical way to package bars of chocolate of a certain shape it would be necessary to investigate various possibilities before coming to a decision.[4]

The investigations in this book provide a focus for mathematical discussion and the formation of skills and attitudes which can extend across the curriculum. The development of positive attitudes is a key aim of these activities. Children need to be given opportunities to develop independent thinking, to gain confidence in themselves and in the work they carry out. It is important that children develop positive attitudes to mathematics through enjoyable purposeful activity which brings them success at their own level. Opportunities should be given for them to develop concentration and persistence – as well as to experiment and to be playful. Children should be given a sense of control over their own learning at a level suitable to them.

The fear of mathematics that many children and adults feel often derives from over emphasis on the 'right' answer. In investigational work we should be encouraging the attitude of 'coming to know', operating, experimenting and modifying things we are trying to understand and use. Investigational work allows for problem posing as well as problem solving – 'What is the problem really saying?'

'What if we look at this part?' And after a problem has been solved a new set of questions arises – 'What is the result of my solution?' 'What way can I do it differently?' In a situation where we are asked to investigate problems, to pose questions or to modify what has been given, there is no one right question to ask, simply an infinite number of questions that could be asked. An open-ended investigation which involves problem posing can be harder and more rewarding than finding one right answer to a problem.

For example, look at this shape:

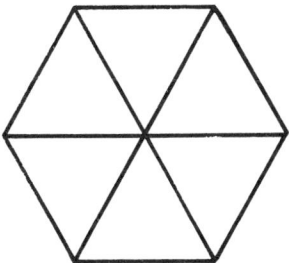

What questions could you ask about it?
What problems could you pose or investigate?
(Is it six equilateral triangles? A hexagon? The top of a tent? Design for a pouffe? A cube? Two cubes in one? What are its dimensions? Does it tessellate? etc.)
Investigational work is founded on the premise that we understand something best by using it, by playing with it, exploring it, changing it – by making it our own.

The aim of *Investigating Maths* is to provide children with a rich and enjoyable experience involving appropriate knowledge skills and concepts related to their ability and aptitude. The activities will provide opportunities to encourage independent study skills, as well as the social awareness of working co-operatively on a project with others (other children, but also parents and teachers). Investigational work can also introduce the aesthetic elements of mathematics: an appreciation of the order, beauty, pattern and design of shape and number. Investigations provide for the possibility of an in-depth study of mathematics through the extension activities suggested in each unit. Each unit provides a challenge which will give children a sense of achievement as well as extend their conceptual development.

1   For more on problem solving, see *Problem Solving in Primary Schools*, ed. Robert Fisher (Basil Blackwell, 1987).
2   Adapted from *Thinking Things Through* by Leone Burton, chapter 4 (Basil Blackwell, 1984).
3   Department of Education and Science, *Mathematics Counts: Report of the Committee of Inquiry into the Teaching of Mathematics in Schools*, chairman W.H. Cockcroft (HMSO, 1982).
4   Department of Education and Science, *Curriculum Matters 3: An HMI Series, Mathematics from 5 to 16* (HMSO, 1985), para. 4.12.
5   *Mathematics Counts*, para. 249.

Skill	1	2	3	4	5	6	7	8	9	10	11	12	13	14	15	16	17	18	19
Calculating	✓	✓		✓	✓	✓	✓	✓	✓		✓	✓		✓					
Charts and diagrams	✓					✓	✓		✓	✓	✓								
Commutativity	✓			✓					✓		✓								
Conservation			✓					✓					✓						
Counting	✓	✓	✓		✓			✓	✓		✓		✓		✓		✓		✓
Describing			✓		✓		✓		✓	✓			✓	✓				✓	
Drawing/folding			✓	✓		✓		✓		✓					✓	✓		✓	
Estimating															✓	✓			
Following rules		✓			✓	✓		✓		✓	✓		✓		✓				
Matching				✓													✓		
Measuring					✓		✓												
Notation/symbolisation		✓				✓	✓			✓		✓							
Place value							✓							✓					
Prediction/testing/generalising	✓	✓	✓	✓	✓	✓	✓	✓	✓	✓	✓	✓	✓	✓	✓	✓	✓	✓	✓
Rotation				✓												✓			
Spatial orientation			✓	✓						✓		✓	✓	✓	✓	✓	✓		✓
Symmetry									✓		✓							✓	✓
Tessellation				✓															

Summary Chart Book 1

Topics	Area	Weight	Volume	Length	Money	Time	Number	patterns	fractions	Plane shape	Solid shape	Angles	Routes	Probability
Super Cones				✓			✓							
Domino squares							✓	✓		✓				
Mazes										✓		✓	✓	
Halve it!	✓				✓				✓	✓		✓		
Guess and test						✓	✓		✓					
Frogs and Toads														
Helping the Post Office		✓			✓		✓	✓						
Cut the cake	✓						✓	✓	✓	✓				
Cube shapes	✓		✓				✓	✓			✓			
Crossing the river														
Jumbo and the buns							✓			✓			✓	
Race track							✓							✓
How many ways?							✓	✓						
Poison							✓	✓						
Tick all							✓							
Mind reading				✓								✓		
Getting the right angle												✓		
Factory							✓							
Tracing puzzles												✓		
Peg patterns							✓	✓						

Equipment   Red and brown pencils or crayons, paper or pupils' worksheet, a collection of coins

Facts that will aid investigation   Vocabulary: Cone, scoop, flavour

Skills   Logical analysis of possible combinations, addition of 5, 7 and 9 in units of three

Concepts   Combinations of three elements

Teaching points

Children may draw their results on paper or the pupils' page, or write the combinations down (for example, VSC = vanilla, strawberry, chocolate). You may need to explain how buying a cone with vanilla, strawberry and chocolate is the same as buying chocolate, vanilla and strawberry: it is not the order of scoops that matter, it is the variety. You may wish to leave the children to discuss this and decide it for themselves. Ask, 'How many cones contain only two flavours?' The price of each Super Cone can be recorded on the dotted lines by each cone.

Children may like to cut out their 'cones' and 'scoops' from gummed paper in the appropriate colours and stick them onto paper. Children may also like to investigate variations of two scoops from three flavours, four scoops from four flavours, etc. See if they can predict what the answer might be. Ask the children to check their answers with a friend.

Extension activities

1 Ask children to investigate their own prices for each flavour.
2 Add an element – for example, one or two chocolate flakes – and investigate the effect on variety and price.
3 Explore ways of spending certain amounts, e.g. 25p.
4 Other investigations
   a 'The bucket puzzle' How many different ways can you colour the three stripes on a bucket – using up to three colours?
   b 'Flags' Explore the colour combination on flags, such as the Union Jack or a flag of the child's own design.

Related investigations   'Eggs in a box' (Book 3), 'Colouring squares' (Book 4)

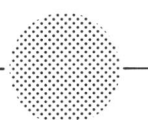

Investigating Maths

1 Super Cones

What you need: Two coloured crayons, red for strawberry, brown for chocolate. Vanilla is white so you do not need to colour it.

The ice cream man sells Super Cones. Each one has three scoops of ice cream. There are three flavours to choose from: strawberry, chocolate or vanilla.

1 Colour in the strawberry and chocolate scoops in this picture.

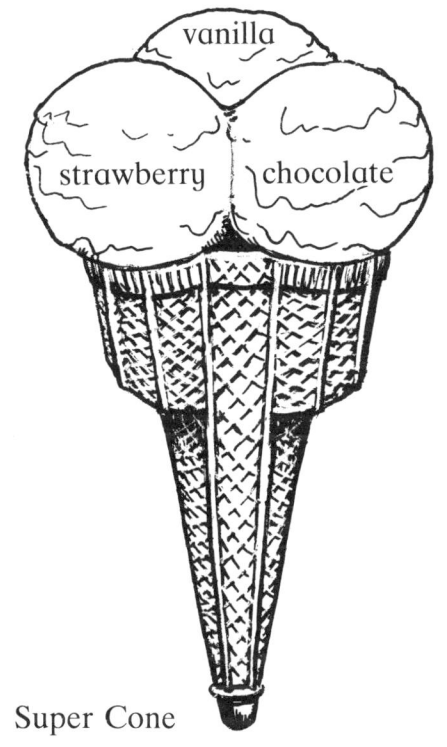

Super Cone

2 Find out how many different cones the ice cream man can make with his three flavours.

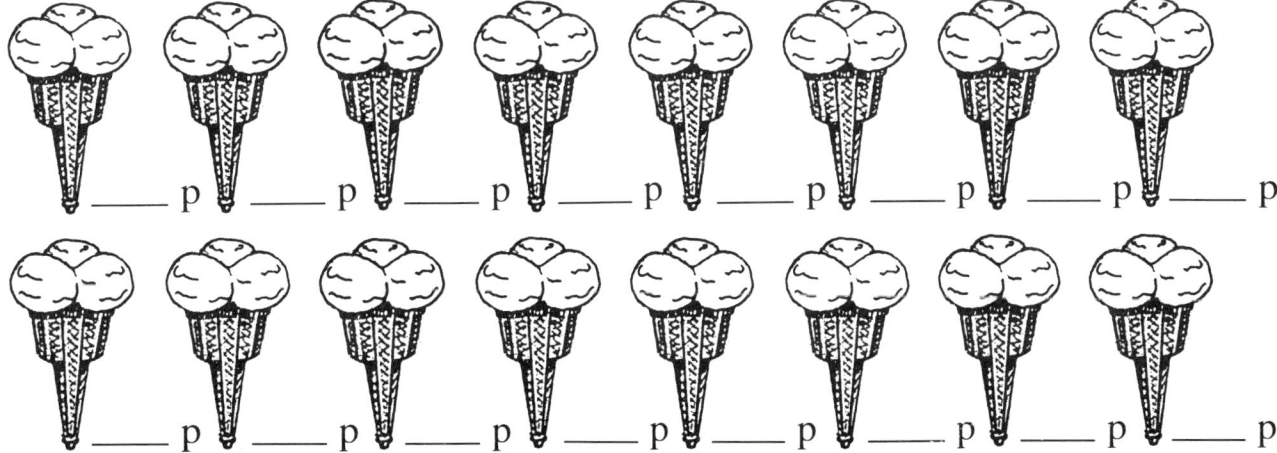

3 Vanilla costs 5p a scoop, strawberry costs 7p a scoop and chocolate costs 9p a scoop. Find out how much each of your Super Cones costs. Write down the price of each.

Domino squares

Equipment   A set of dominoes

Facts that will aid investigation   Addition bonds up to 10

Skills   Addition, test-and-improve strategies

Concepts   Number patterns and sets

Teaching points

Some questions to ask during the investigation:
   'How many different domino squares can you make?'
   'What is the smallest number the spots along each side can add up to?'
(Try the four dominoes with the smallest totals.)
   'What is the largest number the spots along each side can add up to?' (Try
the four dominoes with the largest totals.)
   'Are there any numbers between these two that you cannot get? . . . If
not, why not?'
   Children can be asked to record their findings. Remind them to select
from the whole set each time. A harder task is to see how many separate
domino squares can be made out of one set (the maximum is seven squares).
   Dominoes – representing numbers by patterns of round dots – preceded
the invention of numerals by many centuries. A Chinese manuscript dated
2000 BCE shows the numbers 1–9 as dots, arranged as a magic square. The
game of dominoes can involve many mathematical benefits such as counting,
matching, number patterns, adding and subtracting.

Extension activities

The use of random spot dominoes (available from E.J. Arnold and other
stockists) can prevent stereotyping of one pattern of number, and can give
rise to interesting investigations. How many ways are there of depicting the
number 3 in spots? Children can create their own domino pieces, inventing
their own number patterns. This will involve exploring different designs for
the same number, and perhaps to extending the series to 10 or further.

Related investigations 'Domino bridges' (Book 3)

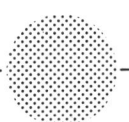

Investigating Maths

2 Domino squares

What you need: A set of dominoes, pencil

1

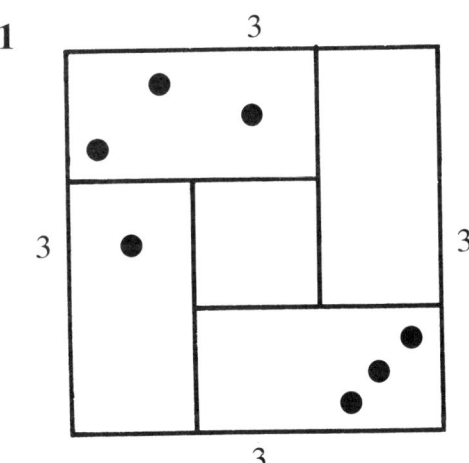

These four dominoes make a **domino square**. It is called a domino square because the spots along each side add up to the same number: 3.

Can you make this domino square with dominoes?

2 Here is another domino square. The spots along each side add up to the same number.

Can you see what number it is?

_____

Make this domino square with your dominoes.

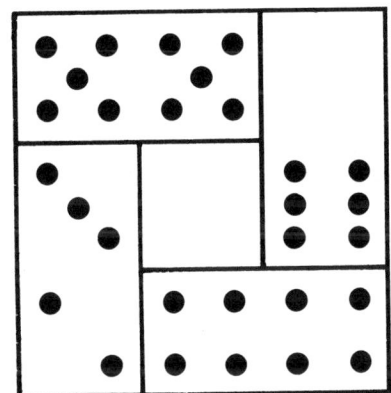

3 Make your own domino squares.

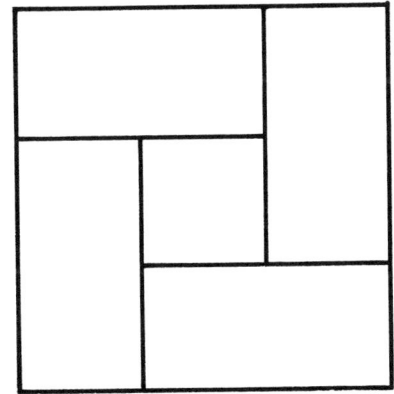

Find four dominoes to make a square. The spots along each side must add up to the same number.

See what other domino squares you can make.

What is the smallest number the spots along each side can add up to?

_____

What is the largest number? _____

Mazes

Equipment Pencil and paper

Facts that will aid investigation Terms: Maze, middle, corner

Skills Topological, finding routes, problem-solving strategies, test-and-improve methods

Concepts Spatial orientation, network routes

Teaching points

Children are fascinated by mazes and the problems they present. A topic on mazes could include the story of Theseus and the Minotaur, collecting and studying maze designs, and visiting a local maze. Maze patterns can be expressed through art, craft, language, number, CDT, PE, music and movement.

Some questions to ask about mazes:
'Can you get through it?'
'Show me how.'
'Describe how . . . '
'Is there only one way?'
'How far do you have to go? . . . In which directions?'
'How could you record the way you went?' (route)
'How would you describe the shapes, lines and directions?'
'Have you been through other mazes like this? . . . How were they different?'
'Could you draw this maze?'
'Could you make a model of this maze?'
'Is it a good maze? . . . Why?'
Discuss strategies for getting through a maze, such as following the left- or right-hand walls.
'Will any one strategy work?'
'What advice would you give someone entering a maze?'
'Have you ever entered a real maze? What happened?'
When children try drawing their own mazes it is often better to encourage them to do a simple overall design, adding 'doorways,' and leave the blocking off of any 'blind alleys' to the end. If they find this too difficult suggest they trace the outline of the rat maze on the pupils' page, for example, and simply modify the layout.

Extension activities

Explore various other forms of routes such as the way from home to school, from school to other local places of interest, from school to nearby towns, and routes around class and school. Ask the children how many ways there are and which is the quickest way. Investigate, record and discuss.

Related investigations The computer program 'Maze',[1] 'Jumbo and the buns' (Investigation 11), 'Tracing puzzles' (Investigation 19), 'Pathways' and 'Routes' (both in Book 2), 'Inside or outside' (Book 3)

1 On the *Microsmile* pack of discs, obtainable from ILEA, Learning Resources Branch, Centre for Learning Resources, 275 Kennington Lane, London SE11 5Q2.

Investigating Maths

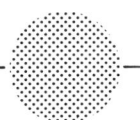

3 Mazes

What you need: Pencil and paper

1 Can you find your way through this maze to the
  mountain in the middle, and then out again?

2 This maze was made for a pet rat.
  Can you show the rat how to get to
  the food?

3 Try drawing your own maze.
  Show where you must start, and
  where in the maze you must try to
  reach.
  Make sure there is a way through
  your maze.
  Then a-maze your friends!

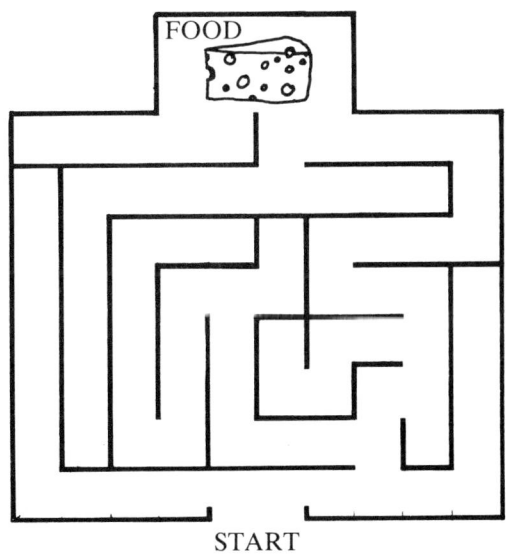

Halve it!

Equipment   Pencil, dotted or squared paper (Resource sheets 1 or 2), ruler

Facts that will aid investigation   Terms: Half, oblong, square, exactly; half of 12 = 6

Skills   Dividing oblongs and squares in half, drawing straight lines

Concepts   Half of something, cutting in half by creating two equal areas in many ways

Teaching points

Children can draw their own bars of chocolate on squared or dotted paper, or use previously prepared oblongs or square bars. They may prefer to colour in their half bars rather than simply draw lines, or cut out their halves to see if they match. Examples of real bars can also be used, or made by the children out of Plasticine, clay or card.

Extension activities

1 Investigate halving bars of different shapes and sizes; for example, 4 × 4, 5 × 5, 8 × 2, 6 × 3.
2 How many different ways are there of 'half-colouring' this shape? (Try to find 13 ways.)

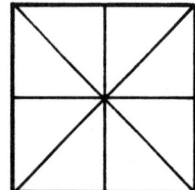

3 Create a class book of 'Halves', showing ways of halving all sorts of shapes, pictures and patterns. Include number facts and measurements, symmetry and reflections and pages of puzzles such as matching halves, etc.
4 Investigate ways of dividing the 'bars' into *quarters*.

Related investigations   'Pathways' and 'Three square' (both in Book 2). See also the computer program 'Take half',[1] 'Curvy quarters' (Book 3), 'Colouring squares' and 'Diagonals' (both in Book 4)

---

1   On the *Microsmile* pack of discs, obtainable from ILEA Learning Resources Branch, Centre for Learning Resources, 275 Kennington Lane, London SE11 5Q2.

Investigating Maths
Name _____

4 Halve it!

What you need: Pencil, dotted or squared paper

Imagine you have a bar of chocolate. How many
ways can you cut it in half to share with a friend?

1 An oblong bar
Here is a bar of chocolate which is an oblong.

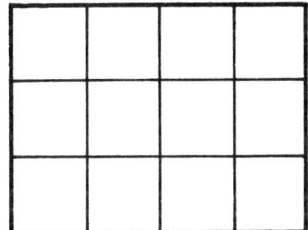

Draw as many ways as you can of cutting it in half.
Here are two:

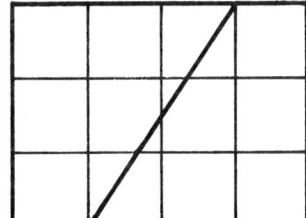 

You can tell if you have really cut it in half by cutting out the
halves and seeing if one half fits exactly on top of the other.

2 A square bar
Here is a square bar of chocolate.
Can you divide it in half by joining the dots with straight lines?

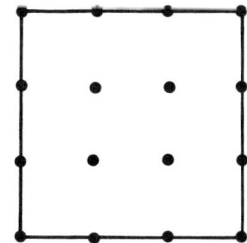

Draw as many ways as you can of cutting it in half.

Guess and test

Equipment   Pencil and clock timer which measures 15, 30 and 60 seconds

Facts that will aid investigation   The measurement of 15, 30 and 60 seconds

Skills   The use of a clock for measuring time

Concepts   The ideas of guessing (estimating), testing, and recording results

Teaching points

The aim is to gain experience in estimating quantities and gathering data. Children should work with partners. Each child guesses how many times he or she can do the activities in the 15-second category. They write their estimates in the 'Guess' boxes, then work with a partner to time one another doing the activities. Then they should compare their 'Guess' and 'Test' columns. When they have finished guessing and testing they should work out and circle their best guess. The same procedure is followed for the 30-second and 60-second questions. Ask the children to compare their test results with their partner. When the children have finished they can try to make up some 'Guess and test' activities of their own.

Extension activities

Do a class survey of these activities. Ask the children to record and to share their own 'Guess and test' activities, perhaps in a class 'Record Book'. Other 'Guess and test' activities could be open-ended, for example by asking:

'How long would it take you to hop 10 times?'

'How long would it take you to write the numbers to 100 (or count by fives to 100, or by twos to 50)?'

'How long would it take you to count backwards from 20?'

'Hold your breath?'

'Write your name and address?'

Children could make up their own time challenges to test on themselves and others. There may be some interesting records to look up in the *Guinness Book of Records*.

Related investigations   'Body maths' and 'String along' (both in Book 2)

Investigating Maths

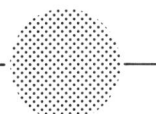

5 Guess and test

What you need: Pencil and a clock timer

First you write your guess, and then you test it with the timer.

In 15 seconds:
How many times could you

tap your foot?

make a fist?

blink your eyes?

snap your fingers?

Draw a circle round your best guess.

Guess	Test

In 30 seconds:
How many times could you

tap your foot?

write your name?

count to 10?

tie your shoe?

Draw a circle round your best guess.

Guess	Test

In 60 seconds:
How many times could you

tap your foot?

How far could you count up to?

How many times do you breathe?

How many times does your heart beat?

Draw a circle round your best guess.

Guess	Test

Can you think of other things that you could guess and test using the clock timer?

Frogs and Toads

Equipment A game board and six counters (to represent three Frogs and three Toads)

Facts that will aid investigation The rules and objects of the game

Skills Step-by-step problem-solving strategies (sequential ordering)

Concepts Spatial relationships, working to rules

Teaching points

This activity can be undertaken on an individual, paired, group or class basis.

As a class activity, arrange six children in seven chairs, three at each end, and ask the children what moves will be needed to swap them over. Record how many moves it took. See if the children can replicate these moves.

Ask the children to suggest ways in which the game can be varied, such as by changing the number of frogs, toads or chairs. Children can use counters on squared paper or pegs or pegboards.

This is an activity which has proved stimulating for children at all stages of schooling. See pp. 41–6 of *Teaching Styles*[1] for ways in which secondary school children have approached this puzzle.

Extension activities

Introduce the rule of no backward moves and ask how many moves it now takes to change over the counters. If children make up their own games, encourage them to vary the rules, or to design their own boards. Ask them if there is another way of doing it.

Related investigations 'Crossing the river' (Investigation 10). See also 'All change' (p. 224, *Problem Solving in Primary Schools*, ed. R. Fisher, Blackwell 1987).

---

1 An ATM discussion book available from the Association of Teachers of Mathematics, King's Chambers, Queen Street, Derby DE1 3DA.

Investigating Maths

Name _____

6 Frogs and Toads

What you need: A board and six counters. You can play on this board, or draw one of your own. You can cut out the counters from the bottom of this sheet if you wish.

This is a puzzle game for one or more players.
Place the three Frogs and three Toads on the
board like this.

The Frogs and Toads want to change places. Can you help
them to swap over to end up like this?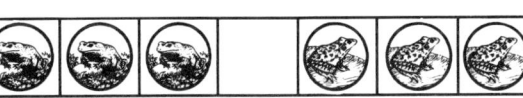

Rules to remember
1 A Frog or Toad can move into an empty space.
2 A Frog or Toad can hop over one Frog or one Toad
  into an empty space.
Can you show how the Frogs and Toads change places?
Show a friend or draw a diagram.

How many moves does it take?   _____ moves
What is the smallest number of moves you can do it in?   _____ moves
When you have finished this game try to make up your
own game of 'Frogs and Toads' with your own board
and counters.

Equipment Paper, pencil, trays or bags, real or plastic money

Facts that will aid investigation Notation of money and recognition of coins, ordering of coins according to value

Skills Adding (more than two numbers), noting patterns and using them to make predictions, testing of these, working on a shared activity

Concepts Place value in base 2, base 4

Teaching points

Preliminary work to this could include discussion on prices of stamps – the difference between the second and first class service, and why the parcel costs considerably more than the letters.

To promote coin recognition and simple counting, ask the children to make up trays or bags containing the coins needed for each column of the table. There are many ways of doing this. Try asking the children to make them using the smallest number of coins. This is a useful exercise in ordering and exchanging. These collections can then be labelled and arranged as column headings, and cards labelled 0 or 1 used to show the result, as an alternative or addition to the table on the sheet.

Questions to ask and promote discussion:

'Why has the table been drawn with the smaller amounts on the right?'

'Why has a zero been used in one column, but not in the other empty columns?' Both these questions are designed to link the children's present understanding of place value to this activity (though in base 2 rather than base 10, in this case). It is the quality of the discussion that is important, not, at this point, the obtaining of correct answers.

'What do you notice about the patterns of 0s and 1s in the 1p column? . . . in the 2p column?' etc. This patterning may help some children to realise that all values can be produced this way.

'What is the most expensive letter or parcel that can be sent?' This will clearly be when there is a 1 in each column: 31p.

Extension activities

Ask 'What will be the next column to the left after the 16p column?' (32p, one more than the previous maximum.)

'Suppose the Post Office ran out of 2p and 8p stamps. How many stamps of each value would Mrs Patel have to allow for each letter, to cater for all values?' (3 – always one less than the base being used, which is now base 4.)

Related investigations 'Tick all' (Investigation 15), 'Stamps' (Book 2), 'Shopping' (Book 3)

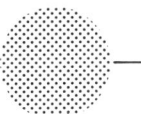

Investigating Maths

Name

7 Helping the Post Office

What you need: Pencil, paper, some friends to work with you

The village Post Office is running out of stamps.
All they have left are 1p, 2p, 4p, 8p, 16p and 32p
stamps. So they are allowing customers to buy only
one of each stamp for each letter.
Some of the villagers are worried.

'Look, I need stamps worth 14p for this
letter, and 30p for this parcel to send to
my grandson for his birthday,' said
Mr Smith.

'Don't worry,' said Mrs Patel, the lady
who runs the Post Office. 'You can do it.'

Was Mrs Patel right? Is there any
amount you cannot make by using
just one of each for each letter?
This table may help you.
The result for 2p is done for you.

Stamps needed for letter	16p	8p	4p	2p	1p
14p					
19p					
30p					
1p					
2p				1	0
3p					
4p					
5p					
6p					
7p					
8p					
9p					
10p					

Cut the cake

Equipment Pencil and ruler

Facts that will aid investigation Terms: Circular, divide

Skills Noting number patterns, prediction and ability to use a ruler

Concepts Areas divided into regions, number patterns, division, intersections

Teaching points

Children will have had much experience of breaking something like a cake, biscuit or bar of chocolate into pieces for sharing with others. 'Cut the cake' is a series of problems which introduces dividing, and involves concepts of the straightness and the intersection of lines (the cuts). The cakes in these problems are circular, but they may just as well have been square, rectangular or irregular. The children might like to cook their own cakes or to make them out of Plasticine to make the cutting more realistic.

To draw the cuts accurately, children will need to know how to use a ruler or straight edge. They may like to try dividing a cake with six or more cuts. The following mathematical progression should arise.

Cuts	Pieces
1	2
2	4
3	7
4	11
5	16

(differences: 2, 3, 4, 5)

Once this progression is observed many other interesting questions can be posed and answered.

'What is the largest number of pieces with 6 or 10 cuts?'
'How many cuts would be needed to get 100 pieces?'

Extension activities

Children might like to try cutting up different shapes. Here are two more to try.

'Slicing the doughnut' How many pieces can you cut this ring-shaped doughnut into with three straight cuts?

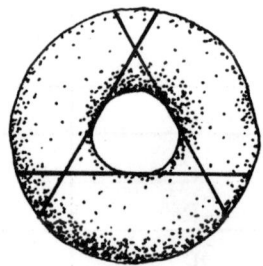

Answer: 9. Here is one possible way to cut it.

Dividing the tart
Mum wants to divide her triangular tart between her four children, so that each gets the same-sized piece. Can you help her?

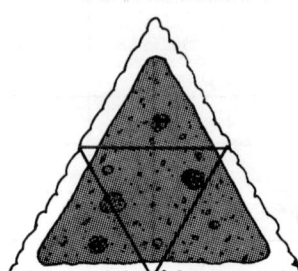

Here is the answer.

Children may like to invent their own shapes to divide.

Related investigations 'Halve it!' (Investigation 4), 'Traffic-lights' and 'Pins and areas' (both in Book 2), 'Circle designs' (Book 3)

Investigating Maths

8 Cut the cake

What you need: Pencil and ruler

You have a cake and knife.
The cake is round or circular.

How many pieces can you divide it into with 1 cut?

_____ pieces

How many pieces with two cuts?   _____ pieces

How many pieces with three cuts?
Draw the cuts on this cake that will
give you the most pieces.

_____ pieces

How many pieces with four cuts?
Draw four cuts that will give you the
most pieces.

_____ pieces

How many pieces can you get with five straight cuts?   _____ pieces
Try your cuts on these cakes, or draw your own.

Cube shapes

Equipment   Forty cubes, preferably interlocking cubes such as Multilink

Facts that will aid investigation   Terms: Cube, shape

Skills   Creation and comparison of three-dimensional patterns

Concepts   Rotation, symmetry, similarity and difference, conservation of volume, ratio, number patterns

Teaching points

Task 1
Questions to use during this investigation might include:
   'Can it make a different shape?'
   'Is it the same shape if you turn it round?'
   'How does this shape compare with that one?'
   'See how many more you can make.'
There are eight possible shapes:

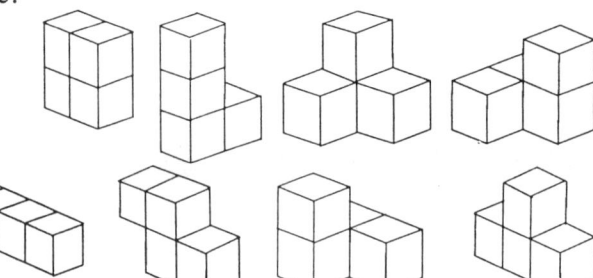

The children may make these in other positions, or rotated versions, and maintain they are different. Show by rotation which shapes are similar, which different. Discussion might include the notion of conservation of volume: 'If these were empty boxes which shape would hold more?'

Children should be encouraged to make many shapes and then to sort them into sets of the same shape. If children get stuck ask them to fix three cubes – for example, in a line – and then try altering the position of a fourth cube until all the possibilities have been exhausted.

Task 2 and Task 3   Discuss the relationship between the number of steps and number of cubes – can the children work out what the next number of cubes should come to in the series before building the steps?

Extension activities

Investigate the shapes you can make with five cubes.
   Explore the possible ways of covering a given area of 16 squares using the five 'two-dimensional shapes' below.

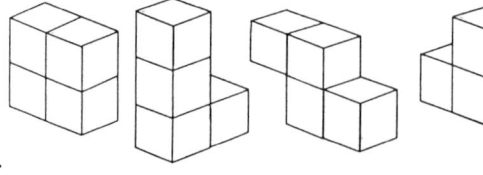

Draw round the shapes on squared paper.

Are there any shapes that do not fit?
   Try making patterns of 16 squares arranged as different shapes. See the examples below.

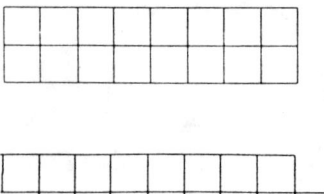
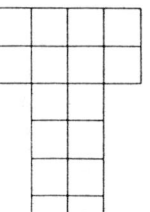
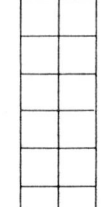
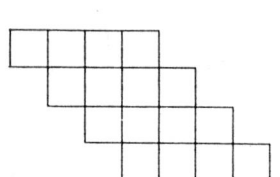

Related investigations   'Traffic-lights', 'Routes' and 'Nets' (all in Book 2), 'Mean Jacko's Treasure' (Book 3), 'Soma cubes' (Book 4)

Investigating Maths

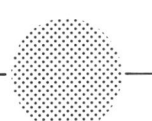

9 Cube shapes

What you need: At least 40 cubes

Use your cubes to solve these puzzles.

1 **Four shapes** Take four cubes and make this shape.
Now take four more and make a different shape.
How many different shapes can you make with
four cubes?

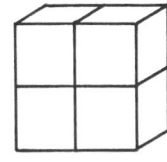

2 **Build stairs** Use your cubes to build these stairs.

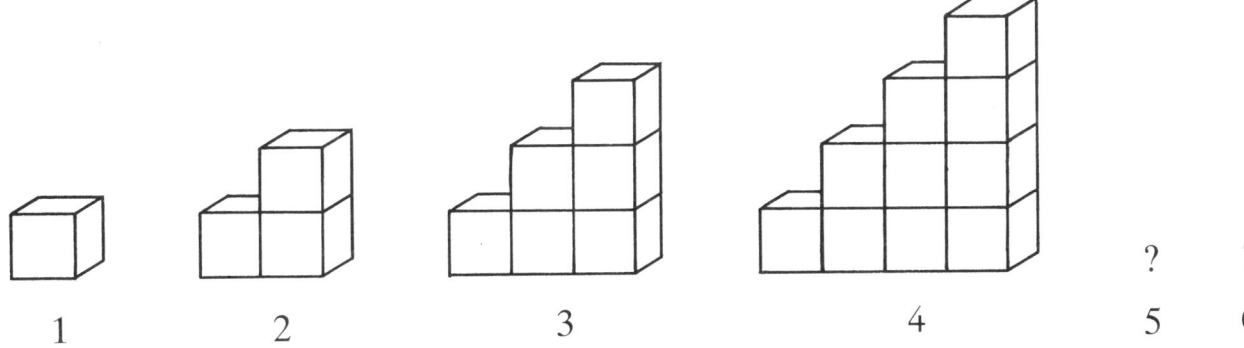

| 1 | 2 | 3 | 4 | ? | ? |
| | | | | 5 | 6 |

Write down how many cubes you used.

Number of steps	1	2	3	4	5	6	7	8
Number of steps	1	3						

3 **Double stairs** Use your cubes to build these stairs.

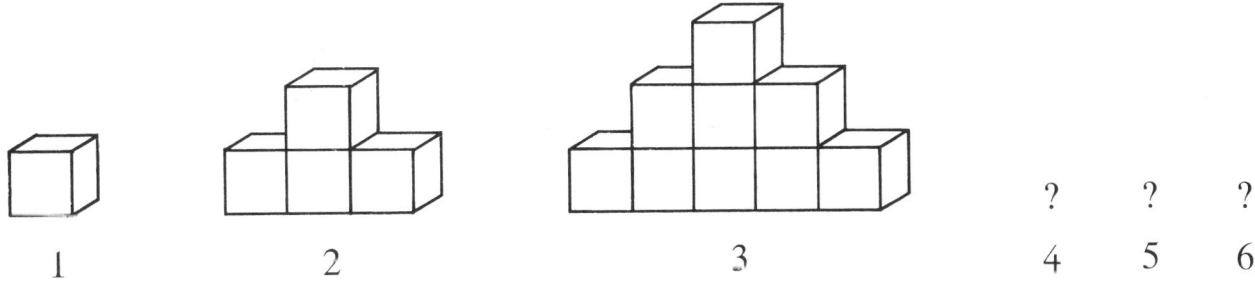

| 1 | 2 | 3 | ? | ? | ? |
| | | | 4 | 5 | 6 |

Write down how many cubes you used.

Number of steps	1	2	3	4	5	6		
Number of steps	1	4						

Crossing the river

Equipment   Pencil and paper

Skills   Problem-solving using, for example, the step-by-step approach, testing hypotheses, abstraction and symbolisation

Concepts   How strategies are needed to solve problems

Teaching points

'Crossing the river' is one version of a very old problem. The earliest written version occurs in *Problems for the Quickening of the Mind* by Alcuin of York (*circa* 775 ACE) and reads as follows:

> A wolf, a goat and a cabbage must be moved across a river in a boat holding only one besides the ferryman. How must he carry them across so that the goat shall not eat the cabbage, nor the wolf the goat?

A simplified version of 'Crossing the river', called the 'Canoe problem',[1] is,

> Two men and two boys want to cross a river. Their canoe will only take one man *or* two boys. How do they all get across?

All classic problems are of interest to people across a wide age range, from infants to adults, and 'Crossing the river' is no exception. It is best tackled as a paired or group effort, as a stimulus for mathematical discussion and activity rather than as a focus for finding the 'right answer'.

Clothing a problem in a story, however simple, can relate mathematics to the real world and to the experience of children. One group of 7-year-olds given this problem spent some time on ways of getting across the river – swimming, being pulled along by the boat, waiting for another boat to come along, etc. Another group discussed why the family wanted to cross the river in the first place. One girl worried how the boatman would get his boat back if it was left on the other bank. Preliminary discussion like this is an important stage in the problem-solving process, providing an opportunity for children to clarify the obstacle and the objective, and helping them to make the problem their own.

What if they get stuck? The first response should be, 'Try it with apparatus.' Use models, cubes, rods, sticks, counters, pieces of paper – anything that will show the problem in concrete form. Another way is to act out the problem: role play the family, the boat and the river.

Extension activities

Encourage the idea that many different approaches to a mathematical situation are possible and acceptable. Children may say, show, write or draw their solutions. Older children might be encouraged to show the solution in its simplest symbolic or pictorial form. Children can also create their own river-crossing problem stories.

Related investigations   'Boat',[2] 'Frogs and Toads' (Investigation 6)

---

1 See Janet Duffin's description of her experience of presenting the 'Canoe problem' to teachers, parents and children, in *Problem Solving in Primary Schools*, ed. R. Fisher (Basil Blackwell, 1987).
2 On the *Microsmile* pack of discs, obtainable from ILEA Learning Resources Branch, Centre for Learning Resources, 275 Kennington Lane, London SE11 5QZ.

10   Crossing the river

Once there was a mother, father and two children
who wanted to cross a river. There was no bridge.
How could they get across?
They saw a man with a rowing boat.
'May we borrow your boat?' asked Mum.
'Yes, you may,' said the boatman, 'but it is only a
small boat. It will carry only one grown-up, or up
to two children at a time.'
'May the children row the boat?' asked Mum.
'Oh yes,' said the boatman, 'and you can leave the
boat on the other side if you wish.'
'Thank you,' said Dad. 'Now we must work out a
way to get across.'
Can you show how the mother, father and two
children can cross the river in their small boat?

Remember that the boat can carry only one adult,
or one or two children at a time. Show your friends
how to do it. Use models or a drawing.

Jumbo and the buns

Equipment   Pencil, paper

Facts that will aid investigation   Knowledge of cardinal number

Skills   Addition of several single-digit numbers, subtraction strategies

Concepts   Less than, more than, optimising, minimising, commutativity of addition

Teaching points

The aim is to investigate and create number mazes. Here are some suggestions for questions to ask the children at each stage of the activity.
'How many rooms are there?'
'How did you find the total number of buns?'
'How can you check to see if you are right?'
'Would it matter if you added the numbers in a different order?'
'How many buns are left?'
'Do any two routes give the same number of buns?'
'How many different routes are there entering 5 (or *n* number of) rooms?'
Ask them to predict, before testing, whether Jumbo will get more buns going from exit to entrance.
Children will often prefer to draw actual buns in their own funhouses rather than the number.

Extension activities

Children can be encouraged to vary their funhouses with the addition of new doorways and rooms. They can change the storyline, for example to monkeys and bananas, squirrels and nuts, or dogs and biscuits. The story can be acted out in a drama session, using roped off areas and props (with coloured string to show the different routes). Three-dimensional funhouses can be built out of boxes, wood or scrap materials.

Buns can be made using 1 cup of flour, ½ cup of salt and water to mix into a dough; shape into small 'buns', then bake at 150° for an hour. These are durable, but please don't taste them!

Related investigations   'Mazes' (Investigation 3), 'Tracing puzzles' (Investigation 19), 'Routes' (Book 2)

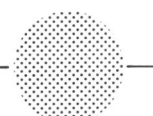

11 Jumbo and the buns

What you need: Pencil and paper

Help Jumbo to find some buns.

Jumbo the elephant has his own funhouse.

Inside the funhouse there are many rooms.

Inside the rooms there are some buns.

(The numbers tell you how many in each room.)

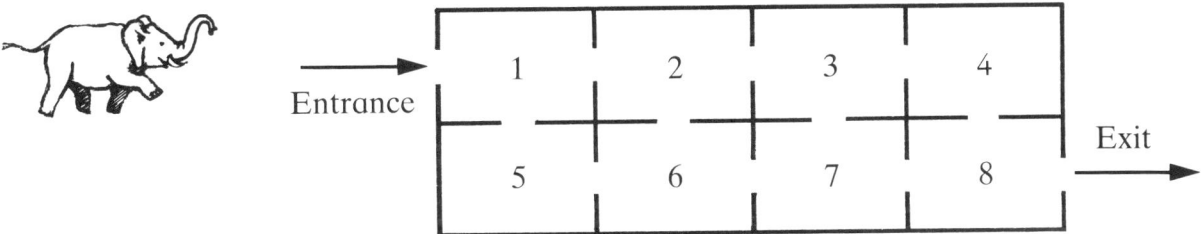

Jumbo must go in at the entrance and out at the exit.

He does not have to visit each room, but he must not visit the same room twice.

How many buns are there in the funhouse? _____ buns

What is the largest number of buns Jumbo can get? _____ buns

What is the smallest number of buns he can get? _____ buns

How many different ways are there for Jumbo to go through

the funhouse? _____ ways

How many buns would he get each time? _____

Would he get more buns if he went in at the exit and out at

the entrance? _____

Draw your own funhouse for Jumbo. Show how many buns there are in each room.

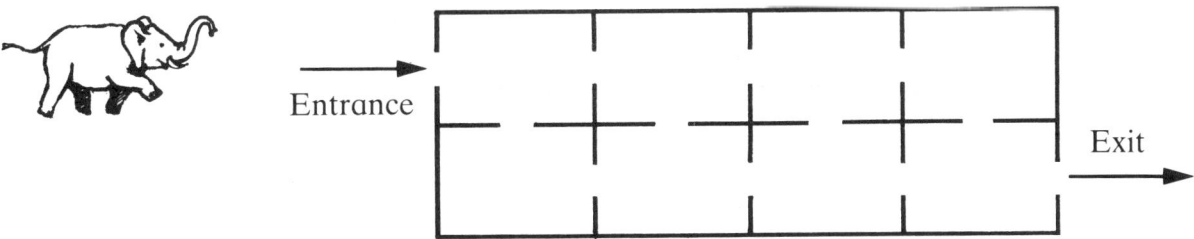

Make up some questions to ask about your funhouse.

Race track

Equipment   Game board (Resource Sheet 3), two dice, counters of various colours

Facts that will aid investigation   Addition bonds up to 12

Skills   Matching dice to cardinal number, addition of whole numbers to 12, practical division with remainder

Concepts   The probability of something happening depending on the number of ways it can be achieved, importance of the size of the sample

Teaching points

This is a game which is enjoyable and exciting to play, and also involves a great deal of mathematical thought: basic ideas of probability, number bond reinforcement, and, in the setting up of the game, division. Playing team against team is a good way to encourage discussion on the best strategies to adopt.

To begin with most children put their counters down in a random fashion, though some realise that they should avoid Track 1. At the end of the game, the board may well look like the example below – a fairly typical probability curve.

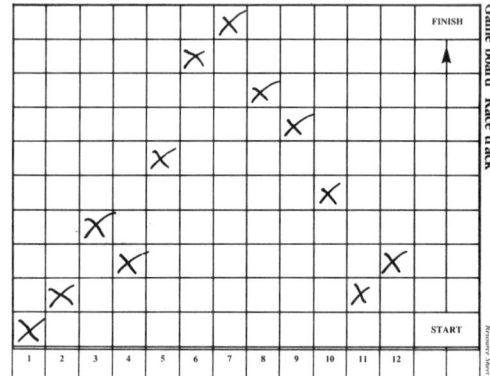

The following questions will help to guide children's observations:

'Why has the counter on Track 1 not moved?'

'Where are most of the best race tracks?'

'Where is it best not to place your counters?'

'Is there any pattern in the way the counters have ended up?'

'Is there a race track which spoils this pattern?' There is usually at least one 'rogue' counter. Discussion could centre around the element of luck in any game of chance.

'Would the pattern have been any different if the race tracks were longer?'

Try extending the board with some 2-cm-squared paper (Resource Sheet 2). The more throws needed, the more likely that the pattern will be as predicted. On the second game, watch to see which race tracks the children choose first, and ask them why they chose them.

Extension activities

Use two blank dice to limit the numbers you can have – say, two each of the numbers 2–4. You can then modify the game to include multiplication of the numbers on the dice (you will have to extend the board horizontally if any number on the dice is greater than 3) or to include zero (adding or multiplying). Dice with more than six sides can help you to extend the game and the degree of difficulty of the addition required. Can the children devise a way of allocating race tracks so that all players have a nearly equal chance of winning?

Related investigations   'How many ways?' (Investigation 13) is very closely connected and can well be used immediately prior to, after, or during this investigation, in order to clarify the concepts involved; 'Dice games' (Book 2), 'Take a chance' (Book 3)

Investigating Maths

12 Race track

What you need: Gameboard, two ordinary dice, counters

You can play this game with some friends. Each player
should have counters of a different colour.

1 Each player puts a counter on any track at the starting
position.
Take turns to choose all the tracks so that each player has the
same number of tracks. Only one counter should be in each
starting position.
Now start the game. Take turns to throw the two dice.
Add the two numbers on the dice. If the number is the
same number as one of your tracks, move the counter
forward one place.
The winner is the first person to get one of his counters
across the finishing line.

2 When you have finished playing, talk about the result.
Is the game really fair?

3 Play again. This time, think carefully about which starting
positions you choose.
When you have finished this second game, talk about what
you have discovered.

How many ways?

Equipment   Multilink, Unifix cubes or similar, and paper

Facts that will aid investigation   Number bonds

Skills   Bracket notation, tabulation of results, number pattern recognition

Concepts   Idea of 'ordered pair', predicting from specific examples

Teaching points

We have chosen to make ordering of the pairs of numbers relevant because this makes a simple pattern of the number of ways possible for each stick: the results being the whole numbers in ascending order. Also, it introduces the idea of the ordered pair, an important concept met quite early on in the primary years through coordinates. The bracket notation $(1, 3)$ is preferred to the notation $(1 + 3)$ for this implies commutativity. The children may well be ready to inform you that $1 + 3$ is the same as $3 + 1$! Questions to ask:

'Why must we write the results like this?' (See above.)

'Can you see a pattern in your results?'

'How can we use this pattern to find answers to ways of splitting large sticks?'

It is important to emphasise that predictions should be checked. A 12-cube stick could easily be checked practically. If the results confirm the prediction then it is reasonable to assume that the perceived pattern will continue. Note, however, that we have not proved that the pattern holds for all cases, but simply established a rule that seems to work.

The penultimate paragraph is designed to link this activity to 'Race track', the six cubes corresponding to the six numbers on a die. This leads to results similar to above, up to a 7-cube stick; after that, the number of ways reduces until there is only one way of splitting a 12-cube stick, and this directly relates to the probability of winning the race.

Extension activities

Ask the children, 'Is it possible to split a 10-cube stick into two sticks that have a 4-cube difference in height?' (Yes – $(7, 3)$ and $(3, 7)$.) 'Can it be done with a difference of 3, or 5?' (No – try it for yourself!) 'Can you get these differences using a 9-cube stick?' This sort of questioning and activity is designed to lead to the general rule that a stick with an even number of cubes can only be split to give an even difference, a stick with an odd number of cubes can only be split to give an odd difference.

What pattern is produced if order is not taken into account? (See first paragraph.)

Related investigations   'Race track' (Investigation 12), 'Bombardment' (Book 3)

Investigating Maths

Name _____

13 How many ways?

What you need: Ten Multilink or Unifix cubes, paper and pencil

1 Join 4 cubes together to make a stick. How many ways
can you split this into two? You should find three ways.

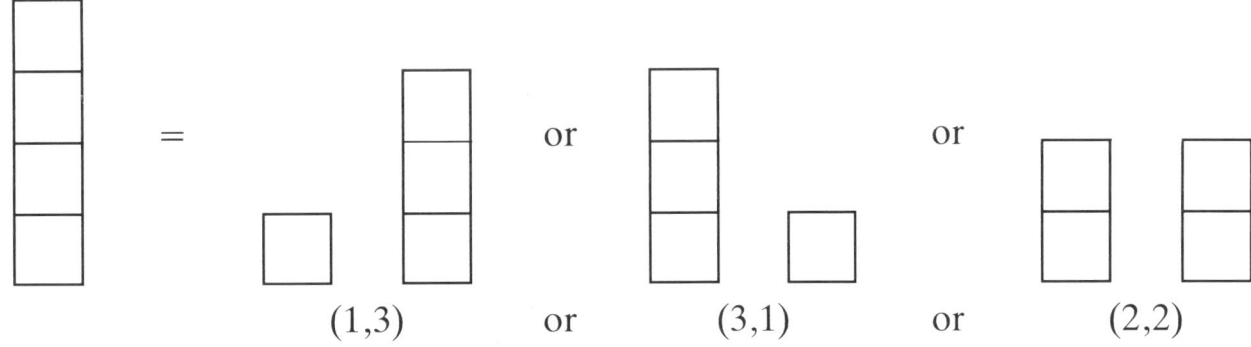

(1,3)   or   (3,1)   or   (2,2)

2 Try this, starting with different numbers of cubes.
Record your results like this:

Number of cubes in stick	Number of ways of splitting into two sticks
1	0
2	1 (1,1)
3	2 (2,1), (1,2)
4	
5	
6	
7	
8	
9	
10	

Can you see a pattern?

How many ways could you split a 12-cube stick? _____

How many ways could you split a 20-cube stick? _____

3 Say you can only have sticks with 6 cubes or less in your answer.
What is the longest stick you can start with?

A stick with _____ cubes
How are your results different now to your first ones?

Poison

Equipment   Ten cubes, counters, sticks or blocks – or pencil and paper

Facts that will aid investigation   Addition and subtraction bonds up to 10

Skills and Concepts   Problem-solving skills and strategies including prediction, planning, test-and-improve methods, working backwards, making and testing hypotheses, looking for patterns, proving and disproving

Teaching points

The aim of this game is to investigate strategies needed to win. When the game has been played several times using different objects, then squared paper can be used to play. Following this the game could be played using numbers. A calculator can be used to test the prediction of outcomes. The game can be played as a class activity using real children as the 'counters', and with group teams.

Questions to ask could include:

'What happens if you can choose one or two sticks each time?'

'If you have eight sticks left, how many will you take to make sure you win?'

'Can you invent your own rules for a game of "Poison"?'

The children may discover the way to win every time if they are guided through the following strategy:

'If you leave *one* for your opponent, you win. If you leave *two*, who will win?' (Your opponent, by taking only one.) 'If you leave *three*, who may win?' (Your opponent, if he or she takes two.)   'What about if you leave four?' (You will win, because your opponent will have to leave you two or three.)

The player who leaves four, or seven, should win each game. The children may be asked, 'Who should start the game, if you want to be sure to leave your opponent with seven?' (The opponent. If he or she takes one, you take two; if he or she takes two, you take one – and you should win every game!)

Extension activities

1 'Take the last'. Put a single pile of small objects such as counters, coins or beads on the table. Decide the maximum number that can be taken at any one turn (up to 10). Each player takes up to this maximum number from the pile, in turn. The player who takes the last object is the winner – or loser (decide first!). Is there a way of winning each time? What happens if you work backwards from the problem? Work out the strategy to win each time.

2 'Nim' is usually played with this formation at the start:

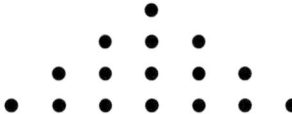

Players take turns to pick up one or more objects from any one row. The loser (or winner) picks up the last object. Tactics? Variations? Recording the games?

Related investigations   Other games, including 'Tactix' and 'Kayles', appear in *Problem Solving in Primary Schools*, ed. R. Fisher, Basil Blackwell 1987.

Name _____

14 Poison

What you need: Ten cubes or counters

This is a game for two players. Two players have
ten cubes or counters between them. Set them up in a row.

The first player takes one or two counters from the row.
The second player does the same.
Take turns to pick up the counters.
The last counter left is the 'poison'.
The player who is left with the poison is the loser.

Play some games with your partner and see who wins.

Can you work out a way to win every time?
Does it matter if you play first or second?
What happens if you begin with fewer counters?
Or with more counters?
What happens if you can choose to take three counters each time?

Tick all

Teacher's Notes

Equipment Paper, pencils

Facts that will aid investigation Knowledge of addition bonds, use of multiplication tables

Skills Multiplication and addition

Concepts Place value in different bases

Teaching points

This investigation is closely related to 'Helping the Post Office', but goes further, using more bases, and by referring eventually to base 10.

The initial activity allows for some experimentation, practice in skills, and to get a feel for the task. The children are then directed towards the economy of using one tick only (or none at all) in each column, and the complexity of using only one column. The least number of ticks is 4 (1×16, 1×8, 1×2, 1×1); the most is 27 (27×1).

Experience of other numbers in this way can be enriched by such questions as,

'Can you make your number, using only one tick in each column like you did for 27? . . . Which way seems easiest to use?'

Practice and discussion should enable children to work out that the highest number possible with only one tick in each column will be 31, and that all numbers up to that can be made in this way.

Having investigated base 2, we may turn to base 3 (Task 2). By referring to the previous questions the children will discover that you need to allow up to two ticks in each column, and that the highest number obtainable by keeping to two ticks is 26. Base 4 requires up to three ticks and the highest number is 63. Questions can include,

'What do you notice about the way the column headings increase each time?' (You could certainly bring the word 'base' in here with reference to this.)

'In base 2 you only needed one tick to be able to show all numbers; in base 3 you needed two ticks – What's happening here? . . . Does it work for base 4 too?'

Now is the time to get the children to have a go at the base 10 example. On noting that you need up to nine ticks in each column, you should get some 'Aha's. Note that you can produce high numbers very easily with this base, but also ask them why, as this is the case, we don't use a higher number for normal counting. Reference to fingers and thumbs should help the penny to drop!

Extension activities

Can the children work out the next column heading to the left in each base, and can they see the relationship between this and the highest number obtainable? Once a base number of ticks is reached in one column it should, in the interest of economy, be exchanged for one tick in the next column to the left; this idea can be reinforced by the use of multi-base apparatus. This is a good way of introducing such apparatus to children. The children can be encouraged to pose their own problems with the material.

Related investigations 'Helping the Post Office' (Investigation 7), 'Strips' (Book 2), 'Calculator number patterns' (Book 3)

34

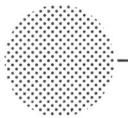

15 Tick all

What you need: Paper, pencils

1 You can work with some friends on this.

Each line of ticks in the table below gives us the number 27.

Line A has two eights (= 16), two fours (= 8), one 2 and one 1.

$$16 + 8 + 2 + 1 = 27$$

Check to see if line B also equals 27.

	16	8	4	2	1
A		✓✓	✓✓	✓	✓
B	✓	✓			✓✓✓
C					
D					
E					
F					

Find other ways of making 27, and write them in lines C, D, E and F.

Which line used the smallest number of ticks?   _____

What is the largest number of ticks you could use?   _____

Try with other numbers on another piece of paper.

What is the highest number you could make with only

one tick in each column?   _____

Are there any numbers that you cannot get using only

one tick in each column?   _____

2 Here are some different numbers.

$$9 \qquad 3 \qquad 1$$

Set them out as a table on a separate sheet of paper.

What is the smallest number of ticks you can have in each column
to be able to make all the numbers from 1 to 26?

3 Now try it for these numbers.

$$16 \qquad 4 \qquad 1$$

4 And these.

$$100 \qquad 10 \qquad 1$$

Mind reading

Equipment   Paper, pencils, ruler, Resource sheet 4

Facts that will aid investigation   Names of simple plane shapes, vocabulary of position, and size

Skills   Identifying and orally conveying properties of shapes and lines, ability to build and record images of these from purely oral instructions

Concepts   Development of vocabulary used will define the concepts in this unit.

Teaching points

This is an effective way of refining children's concepts, involving accuracy of language and imagery. Accuracy of drawing a straight line or a perfect circle are not key issues here. More important is accuracy of description. Graphical recording skills will also be developed.

The main teacher input should be at the discussion stage, focusing on the vocabulary to be used. Such questions may be:

'What do we call a straight line drawn from one corner of a rectangle to the opposite corner?'

'This line here goes in the same direction as this one, like railway lines. What do we call lines like this?'

Precision in the use of vocabulary is important in defining a concept for a child. Terms which will arise may include: parallel, diagonal, circle, triangle (possibly also right-angled, equilateral, isosceles, scalene), oblong, square, rectangle (not forgetting that a square is a form of rectangle; 'oblong' precludes the square), spiral, rhombus, opposite, touching, half-way, and centre.

It is important not to overload the child. Choose just one or two items in each picture to comment upon.

Extension activities

Similar pictures designed to extend the vocabulary can be prepared. Simplified versions that concentrate on fewer concepts can likewise be prepared if required. Children can produce their own sets of pictures; this is a very valuable exercise, for they will have to ensure that they have the necessary vocabulary to describe the pictures.

Other possibilities could be the inclusion of number. An example question could be, 'Each odd number less than ten is in each corner of my shape. Draw the shape and put in the numbers.'

Related investigations   'Pretty Polygon', 'Try angles' (both in Book 2), 'Bombardment' (Book 3)

Investigating Maths

Name _____

16 Mind reading

What you need: Resource sheet 4, plain paper, pencils, ruler and partner

You and your friend are going to help each other make copies of mathematical pictures.

1 Look at Resource sheet 4 to give you some ideas to start with.

2 Choose a picture to describe.
Do not let your partner see it.

3 Say what kind of frame it has around the outside.
(The first one is a square.)
Say how big you think the frame is.

4 Ask your partner to draw the frame, without seeing it.

5 Say what sort of shapes are in the picture and ask your partner to draw what you describe. Say where the shapes are and how big they are.

6 Compare your picture with the one your partner drew.
Are they very different?
Could you have described it in better ways?
Talk about it, then try another picture.

7 Ask your partner to draw a picture in an empty frame on the sheet without seeing it.
See if you can draw the picture from the way your partner describes it.
How good are you at mind reading?

Getting the right angle

Equipment Various sheets of old paper (including torn ones), scissors, paper for making notes

Facts that will aid investigation Terms: angle, triangle, circle

Skills Precise folding, identifying and testing right angles

Concepts Angle as an amount of turn, and as a measurable dimension; right angle as a special case

Teaching points

This activity should be tackled before 'Try angles' and 'Pretty Polygon' as it is a preparation for them, introducing or reinforcing the concept of right angle.

It is essential that children see that angle is an amount of *turn*, independent of length. As a class or group lesson, have one child with his arm held out in front of him, making turns, followed by yourself. Ask children if there is any difference in the amount of turning caused by the fact that you have the longer arm.

Children are often quite surprised to find that the orientation of the original fold in the paper is immaterial and that you can make a right angle in the way described using any shaped piece of paper. Whilst discussing and testing this, children are involved in developing spatial awareness and in developing the concept of angle as a measurable dimension. The final activity is to give practice in identifying static right angles, and testing their predictions.

Extension activities

1 Ask the children to try cutting out triangles, circles or other shapes from paper and see if they can still make right angles.
2 Demonstrate turning through multiples of right angles.
3 Ask children to turn through two right angles and then to use two right angle measures side by side to show this as a straight line.
4 Similarly, four right angles show a complete turn. Children could look for examples of two right angles around them and note them as they did for a single right angle.

Related investigations 'Try angle' and 'Pretty Polygon' (both in Book 2), 'Colouring squares' and 'Clockwise' (both in Book 4)

Name

17 Getting the right angle

What you need: Several pieces of paper, scissors

1 Stand up and face one wall of your classroom, then turn so
that you are facing one of the walls joining the first one.

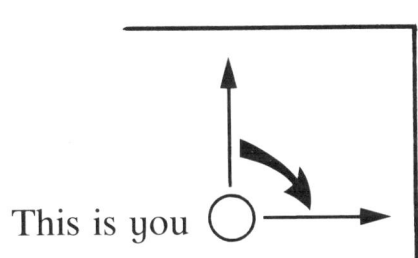

This is you

You have now turned through a **right angle**.
Does it matter whether you turn to the left
or the right? Discuss this with a partner.

2 Now make something to measure right angles, like this:

Take a piece of
paper like this.

Fold it like this.

Then like this.

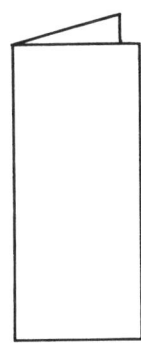

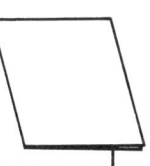

You now have a right angle where the folds meet.
Mark this with a dot.

Does it matter where you made the first fold?
Can you still make a right angle using
a torn bit of paper like this?

A right angle

3 Where can you see right angles in the classroom? Take one of the
right angles you have made, and check the right angles in the room.
Make a list of places where you have found right angles.
Keep your right angle to measure with.

Factory

Equipment   Rods (such as Cuisenaire, or they could be made out of linked cubes), paper, pencil

Facts that will aid investigation.   Representation of number by rods

Skills   Problem-solving skills: Prediction and checking

Concepts   Factors, prime numbers, common factors

Teaching points

Children should already know a colour rod by its numerical name. Make sure that the children realise that each row must consist of identical rods for these to be factors. Saying, 'Three lots of 2', for example, helps to relate factors to multiplication tables.

The notion of a prime number is incidental here and is considered in an investigational way, by posing the question, 'Which other numbers are prime?' and, after giving suggestions and discussion, checking them out practically using the rods.

The results from 1 to 12 are as follows:

Number	Factors	Number	Factors
1	1	2*	1, 2
3*	1, 3	4	1, 2, 4
5*	1, 5	6	1, 2, 3, 6
7*	1, 7	8	1, 2, 4, 8
9	1, 3, 9	10	1, 2, 5, 10
11*	1, 11	12	1, 2, 3, 4, 6, 12

* Prime numbers. (1 is not normally considered to be prime.)

Extension activities

Ask the children, 'What numbers have 2 as a factor? . . . 3 as a factor?' and so on. Numbers that share factors are said to have *common factors*. Ask, 'What common factors are there to the numbers 6 and 12, 3 and 6, and so forth.

Can the children go beyond 12, perhaps by putting rods together to represent higher numbers?

A useful calculator activity is to take any number and divide it by each number from 1 onwards, noting the answers which consist of a whole number only – these will be the factors (as of course will be the numbers they divide by!). Children may well spot that they only need to test numbers up to a certain fraction of the total. For any even number, for example, there are no factors greater than ½ the number except the number itself. How about odd numbers?

Related investigations   'Find the number' (Book 3), 'Diagonals' and 'Spiral table patterns' (both in Book 4)

Name _____

18 Factory

What you need: A set of rods, paper, pencils

What to do: Take a 6 cm rod, two 3 cm rods, three 2 cm rods, and six 1 cm units.
Put the 6 cm rod on the desk and then put the 3 cm rods under it, like this:

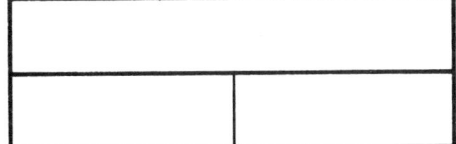

What do you notice?

Carry on downwards, putting the 2 cm rods next, and then the six 1 cm units.

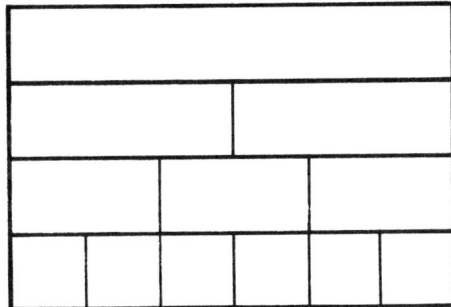

You can see that the 6 cm rod is the same length as:

two 3 cm rods

three 2 cm rods

six 1 cm rods

These rods fit the length of the 6 cm rod exactly. 1, 2, 3, and 6 are called the factors of 6.

Start with a 7 cm rod. Try out the different rods. How many rows can you make? You must not mix up different rods in the same row. What are the factors of 7?

Try this for all the other numbers from 1 to 12.

Some numbers have only themselves and 1 as factors. They are called **prime**. Which numbers from 1 to 12 are prime?

Tracing puzzles

Equipment   Pencil and paper, tracing paper

Facts that will aid investigation   Lines and figures (shapes)

Skills   Drawing, test-and-improve methods

Concepts   Basic properties of two-dimensional shapes

Teaching points

Children enjoy drawing puzzles, and a collection could be included in a class
puzzle box for wet playtimes. Drawing puzzles can also help in the
investigation and discussion of a variety of two-dimensional shapes.
   Questions to ask might include:
'What shape(s) have you traced?'
'Can you trace the shape starting from a different point?'
'If you cannot trace it, can you say why?'
'Can you describe what you are doing while you trace your lines?'
'Can you describe the direction your partner/teacher should trace?'

Some more drawing puzzles to try:

Extension activities

1   Draw four rows of five dots on squared paper.
    Start at any place and draw as many squares as possible without taking
    your pencil off the paper. Without retracing or crossing any line how
    many 'boxes' can you make?

2   As above using five rows of five dots. Work out a scoring system.
3   Old chestnut: Draw three rows of three dots, and then draw four straight
    lines to pass through all nine dots without taking the pencil off the
    paper.   Answer =

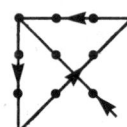

4   Scatter dots over a sheet of paper and get joining!
5   Mark six dots. How many straight lines are needed to join each dot with
    every other dot? Explore different arrangements of dots. Investigate,
    discuss and record.

Related investigations   'Pathways' (Book 2), 'Inside or outside' (Book 3)

Investigating Maths

19 Tracing puzzles

What you need: Pencil and paper, tracing paper

What you do: Use your finger to trace over this figure. You must not draw over any line more than once, or cross over any line.

This shows how you can do it.

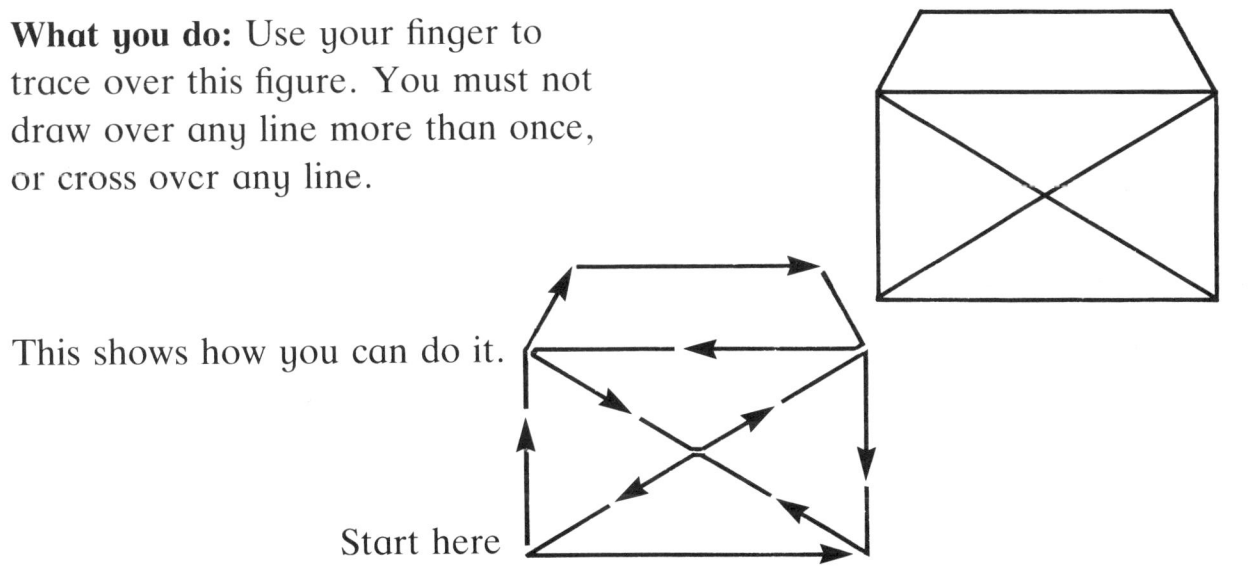

Start here

Trace over these figures in the same way. If you wish, you can trace the figures on to tracing paper. Use the same rules as before.
Start where the arrow points.
Can you do all of them?

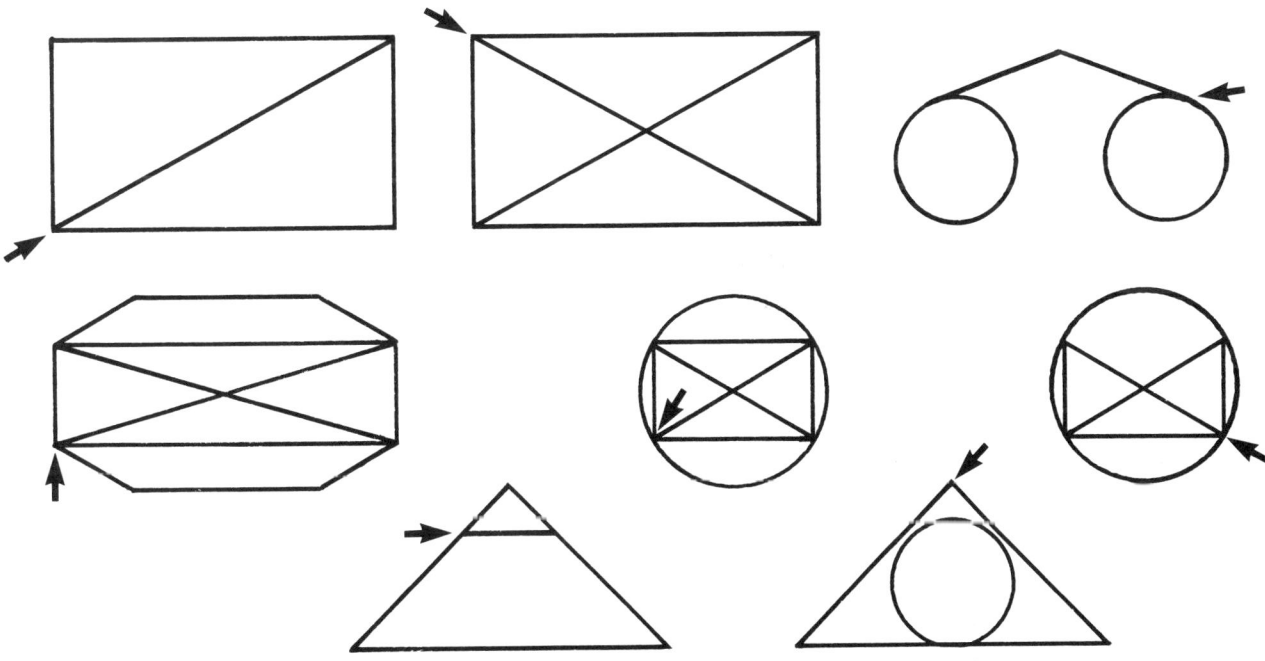

Now draw some tracing puzzles of your own. See if you can trace over your drawing without going over any line more than once. See if your partner can do it.

Peg patterns

Teacher's Notes

Equipment   Pegboards, pegs, paper for working

Facts that will aid investigation   Terms: square, triangle in pegboard form, square numbers

Skills   Test-and-improve, noting patterns in number, prediction and checking

Concepts   Triangular number patterns, relationship between square and triangular numbers

Teaching points

For the first question, only one peg needs to be moved, to produce:

Children should be encouraged to predict the number of pegs required to construct bigger and bigger squares, and to recognize these as the square numbers: 4, 9, 16, 25, . . .

The fact that these numbers can be shown in triangular form often surprises children.

The nine-peg square will need three moves to get this:

– that is 1 peg on the first line, 3 pegs on the second, and 5 pegs on the third. Recognising the 1, 3, 5 pattern may help children to answer the question, 'What is the largest square we could investigate in this way on the pegboard?'

On a 10 × 10 pegboard this would be a 25-peg square which becomes a triangle with 1, 3, 5, 7, and 9 pegs in each row; this would require that 10 pegs be moved. This may be predicted by noting the first three results in the table below. This can be checked practically and the resulting pattern (1, 3, 6, 10) may be recognised as triangular numbers: the difference between each successive number increases by 1 each time.

It should be possible now to work out the answer for larger squares. If further checking is necessary, then two pegboards can be put side by side.

As usual, tabulation of results will assist in investigating this problem and also gives rise to further patterns. For example,

'What do we get if we add any two consecutive numbers in the second column?' or, put in a different way,

'What happens if we take a number in the second column away from its opposite number in the first column?'

The table gives all the answers for squares consisting of up to 100 pegs.

Number of pegs in square	Number of pegs you need to move
4	1
9	3
16	6
25	10
36	15
49	21
64	28
81	36
100	45

Extension activities

1   Use of linked cubes rather than pegs will also work. For example,

becomes   when transformed. With larger examples the children may notice that we are actually splitting a square into two right-angled triangles which are then put together; for example:

2   Investigate how many pegs will be needed to turn a triangle into a square.

For example,   becomes   (1 extra peg)

            becomes   (4 extra pegs)

Related investigations   'Cut the cake' (Investigation 8), 'Traffic-lights' and 'Routes' (Book 2), 'Find the number' and 'Mystic rose' (Book 3)

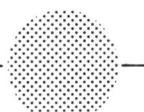

Investigating Maths

20 Peg patterns

45

What you need: Pegboards and pegs

---

1 On a pegboard, make a square with 4 pegs:

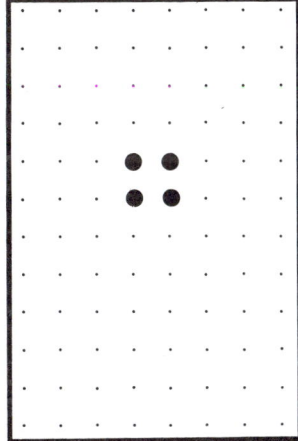

Make your square into a triangle, moving as few pegs
as possible.

How many pegs do you need to move?   _____

2 Now make a bigger square using 9 pegs.
Make this new square into a triangle, moving as few pegs
as possible.

How many pegs do you need to move?   _____ pegs

3 Make some other squares. Turn them into triangles.

How many pegs do you need to move each time?

4 How many pegs would you need to move to make a triangle

from a square made with 25 pegs?   _____ pegs

How many would you need to move to make a triangle from

a square made with 100 pegs?   _____ pegs

Record chart

This chart may be used to record the date on which each pupil completes each activity.

Pupil's name

1 Super Cones																
2 Domino squares																
3 Mazes																
4 Halve it!																
5 Guess and test																
6 Frogs and Toads																
7 Helping the Post Office																
8 Cut the cake																
9 Cube shapes																
10 Crossing the river																
11 Jumbo and the buns																
12 Race track																
13 How many ways?																
14 Poison																
15 Tick all																
16 Mind reading																
17 Getting the right angle																
18 Factory																
19 Tracing puzzles																
20 Peg patterns																

Game board 'Race track'

FINISH

START

1 2 3 4 5 6 7 8 9 10 11 12

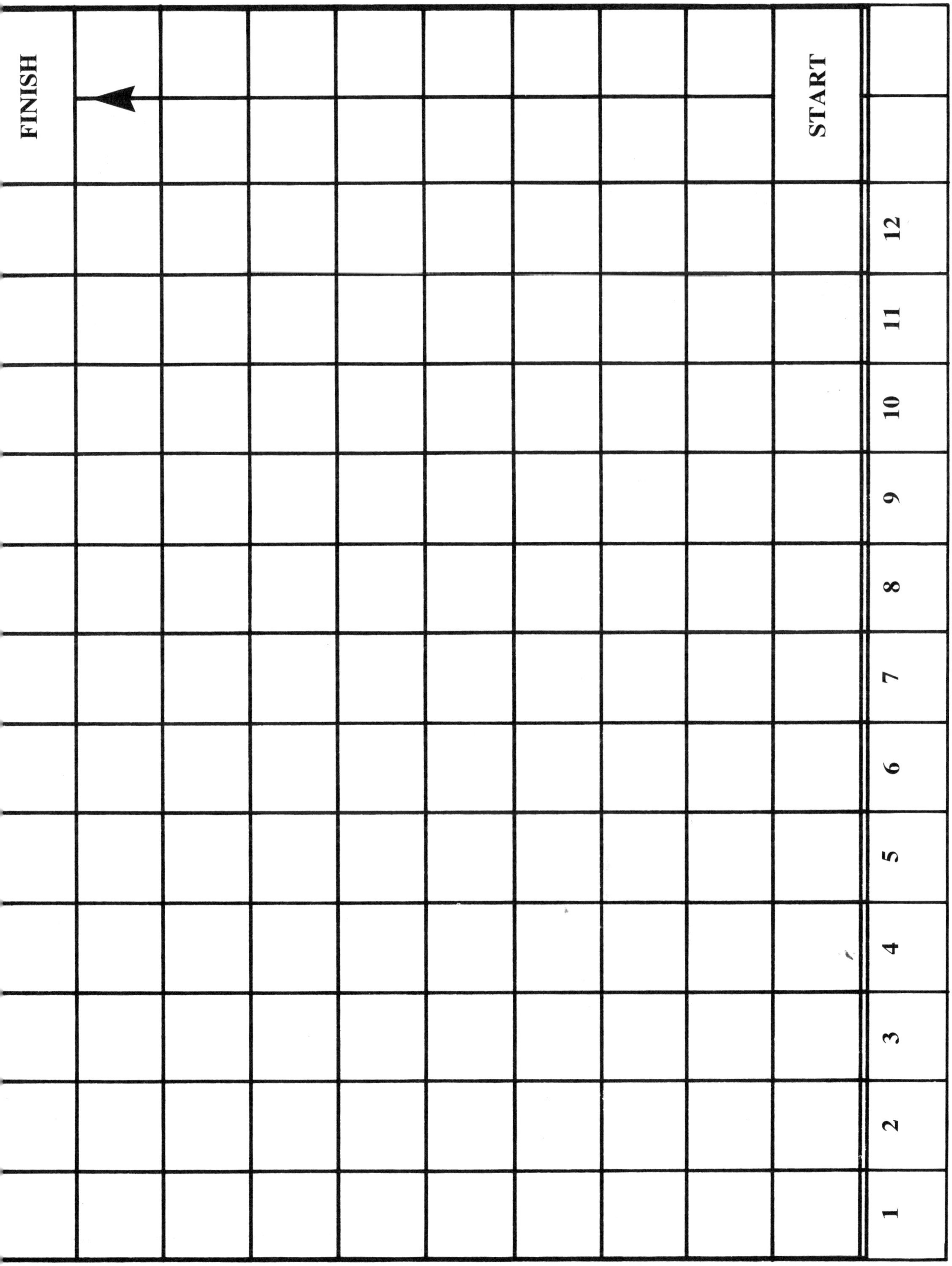

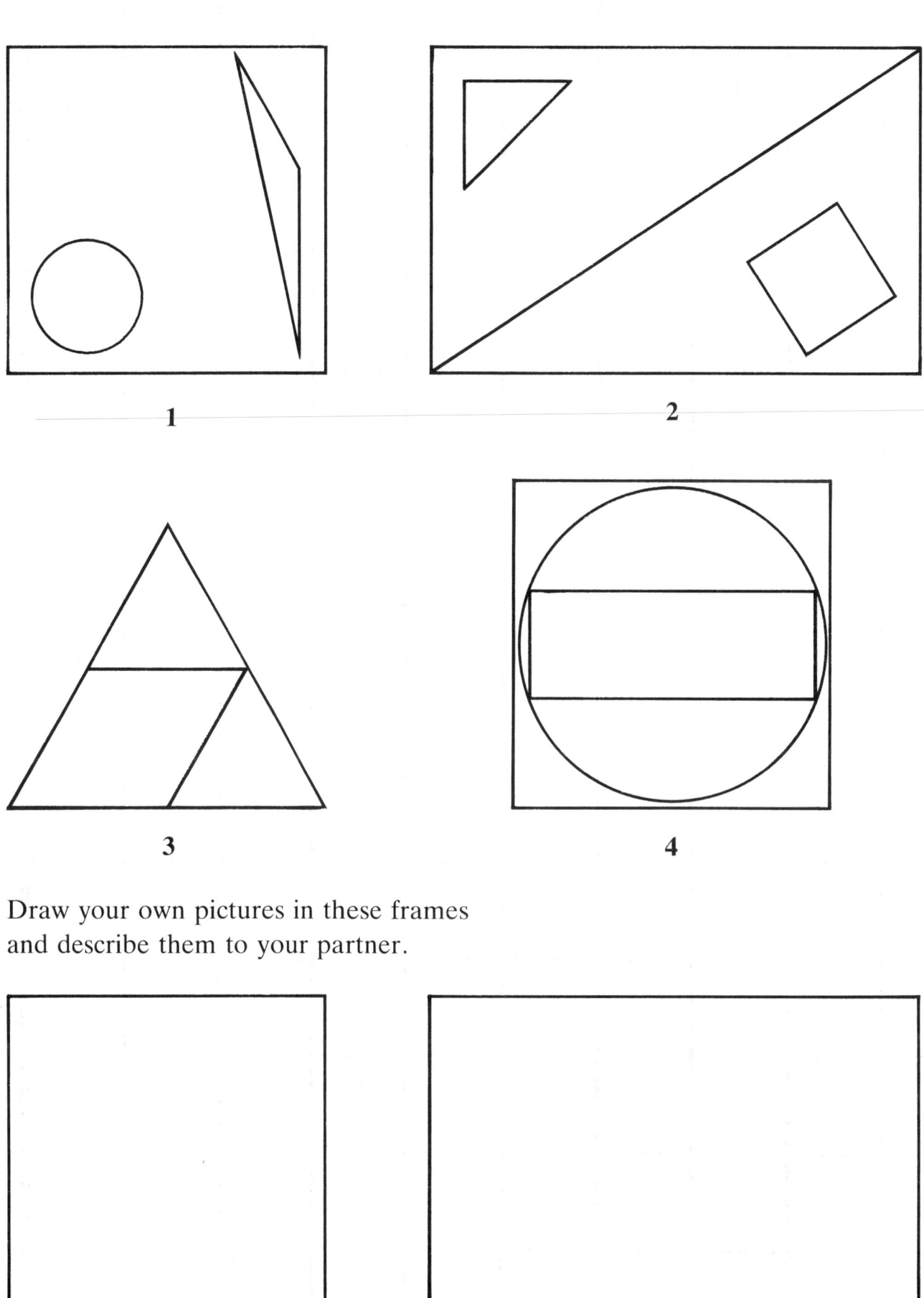

1

2

3

4

Draw your own pictures in these frames
and describe them to your partner.